# An MBA Voyage of Discovery - Deep down the rabbit hole

By
**Professor Dan Remenyi  BSocSc MBA PhD**

First edition, 2014

Softback ISBN: 978-1-910309-31-5
Hardback ISBN: 978-1-910309-39-1
e-Pub ISBN: 978-1-910309-32-2
Kindle ISBN: 978-1-910309-33-9


Published by: ACPIL, Reading, RG4 9SJ, United Kingdom,
info@academic-publishing.org

Available from www.academic-bookshop.com

# Contents

Preface .................................................................................... iii
Acknowledgment.................................................................iv
Dedication ............................................................................iv
About the author....................................................................v
Why tell this story?...............................................................1
First contact with the Graduate School of Business ......................2
Applying to be admitted to the MBA programme......................7
The Formal Interview...........................................................9
The Graduate School of Business....................................... 11
Old Nissen huts...................................................................12
Pre-maths begins ................................................................13
The MBA proper .................................................................14
The MBA ethos and the modus operandi .............................15
The academic calendar .......................................................18
Evaluation of degree candidates' performance......................19
The lecturing team...............................................................20
The A team ..........................................................................21
Other members of the academic team .................................24
The Composition of the Class of '72....................................25
And then the year's work began...........................................28
The relentless treadmill ......................................................30
The Written Analysis of Cases (WAC) ................................31
Impromptu tests and other work challenges .........................32
Conversing with Zeus..........................................................33
Pressure is always only in the mind......................................33
Identify what is really important .........................................34
Social events........................................................................36
Mid-term exams...................................................................36
The second half of the first term..........................................37
The routine grinds on and on...............................................38

Final exams at the end of the first term ........................................... 39

Intellectual achievement at the end of the first term ...................... 39

The results of the exams ................................................................. 41

The second term ............................................................................. 42

New groups ...................................................................................... 44

The Big Shock ................................................................................. 45

The big grind ................................................................................... 47

A pleasant moment .......................................................................... 48

Mid-term exams again ..................................................................... 49

Escaping from the School ................................................................ 49

Intellectual achievement at the end of the second term .................. 50

Apartheid, Protest and UCT ............................................................ 50

The third term ................................................................................. 52

The T- Groups ................................................................................. 52

A computerised business game ....................................................... 54

The second term exam results ......................................................... 54

Visiting faculty and others .............................................................. 56

The pork belly man ......................................................................... 56

The business policy man .................................................................. 57

Rescued by Taylor ........................................................................... 58

The local team ................................................................................. 59

New groups and work loads ............................................................ 60

Excreta tauri cerebrum vincit ......................................................... 61

Intellectual achievement at the end of the third term ..................... 62

Final exams at the end of the third term ......................................... 62

The fourth term ............................................................................... 62

The research report ......................................................................... 63

Job interviews ................................................................................. 64

Intellectual achievement at the end of the fourth term ................... 65

UCT graduation .............................................................................. 66

Finding a job ................................................................................... 67

The Rabbit Hole .............................................................................. 68

Final reflections .............................................................................. 69

# Preface

The story recounted in this book is my personal feelings about the Business School where I obtained my MBA. They are entirely subjective. I expect there will be those who will strongly disagree with the sentiments expressed herein. It is for them to tell their own story.

Even before I set out on my MBA journey I had already heard mumblings and grumblings that the degree was controversial and indeed over rated. "These MBAs think they know nearly everything", was a typical expression. "They think that they deserve to walk into a top job just like that!" was another comment. It is hard to say whether these complaints were justified, but if they were then it was to a large extent employers who found it useful to place MBA graduates in top positions.

And by and large it would seem that most MBA graduates made a success of what they chose to do after their graduation.

The MBA degree is now offered by hundreds if not thousands of universities around the world and this alone is an indication of how well it has done. But MBAs differ enormously and the differences stem from multiple reasons. Resources are obviously critical, as is the prestige of the institution awarding the degree. But there is also the question of the style of the key lecturers and also their sense of responsibility.

The way the MBA was delivered, as described in this book, was a make it up as you go along event and I regret to say that I have seen this attitude operating at other universities in recent years.

This book takes the reader through an educational journey at a particular time and a particular place. Nonetheless it seems to me there may be some general lessons to learn from the story.

## Acknowledgment

As Sir John Tenniel (28 February 1820 – 25 February 1914) has been deceased for more than 75 years his beautiful illustrations for the Alice in Wonderland and Alice through the Looking Glass stories are now in the public domain.

## Dedication

To the memory of Dave Wright who became the Students' Friend during MBA 72.

## About the author

After completing the MBA Dan Remenyi spent 15 years in business as an ICT consultant before undertaking a PhD. Since obtaining his doctorate he has held a variety of visiting professorships in the United Kingdom, the Republic of Ireland and South Africa. He has lectured on a number of MBA programmes. He originally researched and taught in the ICT management field but for the past decade he has increasingly focused on research methodology and the sociology of research. He has had some 30 text books published. Some of his books have been translated into Chinese, Japanese and Romanian. He holds a B Soc Sc, MBA and PhD.

# An MBA Voyage of Discovery – Deep Down the Rabbit Hole

## Why tell this story?

I was prompted to write this book on receiving a copy of the University of Cape Town's (UCT) Graduate School of Business (GSB) Alumni Newsletter in May 2014 in which the following comment was made:-

> *"We were blessed with amazing weather for our three outdoor functions – as well as by the presence of Professor Boland, the first director of the GSB, who taught us so much during our time at the school.................." said alumnus Stewart Cohen (MBA1969).*

I was startled by the use of the word "blessed". This is not a word which I have in my vocabulary and so I looked it up to see what it meant. Well it actually implies some sort of heavenly favour and this made me once again wonder about what the MBA actually did for those of us who invested in the process of obtaining that degree.

At about the same time I met up for lunch with one of MBA '72s graduates and I was told by him that his year at UCT was probably the best year of his life. I was stunned at this comment and it clinched my desire to write this book, which I hope will explain why I find it difficult to understand how it is possible to be blessed by Bob Boland's presence or to believe that the MBA '72 year could be regarded as the best in anyone's life.

It was also around this time that BBC Radio ran a programme called *Short-selling Students* in which they described the current trend of students complaining about the level of service they receive from universities in the United Kingdom. Some universities, it was said during this programme, are not keeping their promises as they should. It appears that the level of complaints has in recent years soared. No official numbers are available although it is believed that today many hundreds of complaints are made. The programme did point out that whereas in the past there were around 30 cases a year considered to be sufficiently serious to reach the courts the number today seems to have rocketed to 70.

The MBA is of course a special event in that it purports to offer a master level education in business studies to highly diverse people in one year. This is generally done without defining a "master level education". Traditionally a masters degree was the bridge between undergraduate programmes and the world of high level academic research as typified by the doctorate. But all this has changed with the taught masters and the structured professional doctorate. This book has been written to provoke thinking around the question, "What is an MBA really about?" And there is no simple answer.

## First contact with the Graduate School of Business

I heard about UCT's new degree in 1968 while I was still an under-graduate at the University of Natal in Durban. There was a poster on the student union notice board informing the campus that there would be a lunch time talk about a new degree which had recently been launched at UCT. The presentation was to be delivered by two Cape Town professors from their Graduate School of Business and this was enough to create some interest. Visiting professors were not a feature of Durban campus life and it was interesting to experience what these people would be like. The talk was held in one of the relatively large lecture theatres and about 30 or 40 people turned up. The

Graduate School of Business of UCT was represented by the two senior professors, Bob Boland and Andre van der Merwe.

It is important to point out that Professor Bob Boland and Professor Andre van der Merwe made quite a dashing pair. Bob was tall slim, spectacled. He was dressed immaculately in a well tailored suit. He was clearly a professional; an accountant as it happened. He wore a smart bow tie and I had not seen anyone wear such a provocative garment before except in the cinema. He had short cut jet black hair and he had an air of professional confidence about him which was quite unlike the staff at the University of Natal. Andre on the other hand was not so slim. A more rounded man in a number of ways he came across as more of an academic. He did not have the sharp edginess that Boland had. He was not as well dressed. His bald head was somehow more human than Boland's shiny black hair. He had a much more approachable manner than Boland. He was a man who could tell an amusing story and still keep his professional poise.

After a brief introduction from a member of the Durban faculty the two professors spoke for about half an hour between them and the message they delivered had five distinct elements which were:-

1. The MBA was new to South Africa (SA);
2. This degree was based on the latest business and pedagogical thinking and practices from Harvard University in the USA, which was by far the most important source of business knowledge;
3. This degree was being taught by the most highly skilled and experienced international faculty who would bring the latest thinking to SA;
4. Only the best young graduates who already had business experience and who were clearly cut out for senior positions in corporate life were being admitted and thus only a small percentage of those who would apply to do this degree would

actually be accepted onto the UCT programme. It was emphasised that working experience was essential before anyone would be considered for admission and thus applicants should be in their mid-twenties.

5. Get a UCT MBA and you are on a fast track to business success.

When I reflect on these statements they sounded too good to be true and at that time I had not yet become aware of the adage that if something is too good to be true then it probably is.

We were told that for those who so wished there was an optional pre-degree maths course and a pre-degree Afrikaans course. The MBA students would be supported in their studies in every way possible.

Being exposed to this performance was a completely new experience. Imagine two professors coming all the way from Cape Town to talk to a bunch of students – nearly all undergraduates. It had never occurred to me that universities needed to sell themselves and I did not take on board that this was a sales pitch.

And when selling their new MBA degree Bob and Andre were quite impressive. They were more like Starsky and Hutch than Tweedledum and Tweedledee. They were clearly quite different people, but they had the same message. The UCT MBA was a tip top degree and it would truly transform you.

There also appeared to be a special collaborative dynamic between Bob and Andre. They, among other things, represented the two major groups in the white South African society and showed the Englishman and the Afrikaner working side by side and this was encouraging. Their performance deserved at least nine and a half out of ten.

There were not many questions raised at the end of their talk, but someone did ask about the costs. The fees were nearly four times the amount that I was paying as an undergraduate and the residence fee was similarly high. But it was pointed out that the degree was a great investment in ones future and that the costs would be easily recovered by the increase in earnings which could be expected after graduation. With regard to funding the degree, UCT had arranged for the major commercial banks in South Africa to lend anyone who was accepted onto the MBA enough money to cover the fees, the year's living costs and out of pocket expenses. And this loan would be at a modest rate of interest and could be paid back slowly after the graduate had found suitable employment.

When the meeting was over a number of those present expressed the view that it would be nice to do that degree someday and some said out loud, "Of course, it will be difficult to get accepted to such a high powered degree, but with a degree like that the sky would be the limit". How pitifully naïve that group was, but then we were nearly all undergraduates after all.

Having finished their presentation and answered a few questions the two professors moved on to their next promotional presentation. They were during this period quite successful in creating awareness of the UCT MBA and in addition to these campus presentations there was some coverage of the new degree in the media.

I soon forgot about Bob and Andre. I graduated a few months after meeting them and went off to work in the field of accounting in a small firm. I had worked with accounts before going to university and so I quickly became the so called "chief accountant" in a small organisation in which I was employed. The exalted title of chief accountant meant that I had two clerks and a secretary with which to produce the monthly accounts, collects the debts, pay the bills, interface with the bank and keep the auditors happy.

Within a few years I was bored out of my mind with this type of work and my thoughts turned to the MBA degree I had been told about and which I had continued to hear about from time to time over the ensuing three years. I was working in Johannesburg and the idea of being in Cape Town for a year was also attractive. Yes, an MBA would get me out of this dreadfully dreary work and put me on a fast track to corporate success. If only I could get into this wonderful UCT programme!

I should say that I was aware that the University of the Witwatersrand (WITS) also had an MBA programme, but their degree required two years of full time study. I could just about have raised enough money to fund the one year MBA and in any event it seemed to me that two years was somewhat excessive. Why take two years at WITS to complete a degree which could be completed at UCT in one? From a business perspective the decision to go to UCT was, what would be described in later years as a "no brainer"! Also the publicity machine in UCT made a good job of making it known that UCT MBA graduates were preferred by employers to WITS MBA graduates. But as a matter of interest as far as I am aware no evidence for this assertion was ever presented.

## Applying to be admitted to the MBA programme

I sent off to UCT for the admission application papers. This was the middle of 1971 and by this stage I had 5 years working experience and was 27 years old.

In what was to me a big fat envelope, the papers arrived in the post. I had never seen an application form like this before. I can't remember how long it was or how many questions there were, but I do recall being intimidated and even startled by some of the issues I was asked about and the type of information I was required to supply. Amongst other things the application form required statements describing a number of occasions in which you have shown your leadership qualities in recent events. It was necessary to write descriptions about how I was able to overcome substantial challenges with which I found myself faced. I was expected to write on subjects such as my strengths and weaknesses and what I would be contributing to the course. I found all this very daunting. If I had not wanted to leave my accounting career so desperately I would not have spent the time and effort on the application form.

I don't remember how many hours I spent on this form, but it appeared to take a very long time indeed to complete. I went through a number of handwritten drafts before attempting to submit anything to print. I had an old portable typewriter left over from an attempt to teach myself typing some years previously. I purchased a new ribbon. I broke up the application form into single pages and fed it into the machine page by page, It took me a number of nights to complete the typing, taking care to make as few errors as possible. This was the time just before *snowpake* erasing was popular and I had a well worn hard rubber eraser in the form of a pencil. I realised after some days of doing this that the penetrating life describing questions were in a sense testing the level of my determination to be admitted as a candidate for this degree. Of course the completed application form also sought to explore if the applicant understood what the thinking of a manager/leader would be in certain situations. I came to the conclusion that the trick was to try to map my experiences onto how I understood managers would think.

The application process also demanded referees who needed to complete a form, place it in an envelope and then sign the back of the envelope so that the applicant could not open it and read it. This of course presented its own challenge. Where was I to find two people who would sing my praises highly enough to convince UCT that I was one of those "best young graduates who already had business experience and who was clearly cut out for a senior position in corporate life" as described by the two professors nearly three years before? I can't remember who I asked to produce references but they must have been kind enough in their opinions of me.

Eventually the application form and the references were completed and posted to UCT.

Then it was necessary to find out how to register for a GMAT (Graduate Management Admission Test). I cannot recall exactly what was involved here or how this was arranged. I only remember that this was another challenge and I ended up taking this test quite late and receiving my results towards the end of the first term at the Graduate School of Business. I recall that it was neither inexpensive nor was it a fun experience and I wondered why I had been put through this process. It seemed to me that the GMAT was a form of American intelligence test with little relevance to me in my environment.

## The Formal Interview

Some weeks after the application form was despatched I was invited to interview for admission to the MBA. I was told that I had to present myself at the Board Room of one of the mining houses in Johannesburg. It was on the top floor of a smart building in the financial area of the city. On arrival I was invited to take a seat in a plush waiting area. The interview panel was running a little late. This was a truly executive environment, I thought. I wondered if this foretold the type of environment I would be working in when I had my MBA?

Some ten minutes later the secretary called me into the Board Room. I was faced by three men sitting behind a large shiny table and a chair was placed on the other side for me directly facing them. These were serious men in suits and I felt that I was now about to be judged. This mining house set up said that the influence of UCT's MBA spread right into the heart of South Africa's industrial might. I wonder what sort of questions would be flung at me. Would I be able to handle this level of adversarial interrogation? Was this going to be really painful?

To my surprise the process of the meeting was completely non-confrontational. It was perfectly calm and quite polite. Nothing was adversarial and the event was not at all stressful. I was informed about how wonderful the degree for which I applied was. I was congratulated on being invited to interview. This meant that I was short listed. I was told that only very good candidates got as far as I now was. I was asked to elaborate on some of the life experiences I had described on my application form. I was asked if I had any questions of my own for them. I was so anxious about this whole process that I couldn't think of anything I wanted to ask. At the end of the interview I was told that I would be informed shortly about their decision.

I went down the 20 odd floors in the lift in the mining house building feeling very positive about my prospects. It looked like they were going to regard me as one of these special young graduates who had the business experience and the potential to be admitted to their fantastic MBA degree.

All I had to do now was to wait for my confirmation of admission. This took some time which at this point seemed to pass interminably slowly for me. I was fully emotionally disengaged from my accounting job in Johannesburg and if I didn't get into UCT for the MBA programme I was not sure what I could have done as an alternative. But in the end a positive letter was received in the post.

I now told my friends and family that I had been admitted to the fabulous UCT MBA. Of course at that time I did not realise just how *fabulous* (in the proper sense of the word) it was going to be. There were congratulations on my obtaining a place on this programme from everyone. It was recognised as an achievement in itself to be accepted for this degree. It was known that this degree was tough but that it would transform anyone's understanding of business and management. I lost count of the number of people who told me that when I had that degree I would be on a fast track to corporate success.

I was then able to make the necessary arrangements to resign. I did not think twice about this, although I did have a couple of friends in the company with which I was employed, and I knew that I would miss working with them. But the prospect of moving to and living in

Cape Town was pleasant. Nineteen seventy one couldn't end quickly enough for me.

## The Graduate School of Business

I was as keen as mustard to get started so I arrived in Cape Town in late December as I had opted to take the pre-degree maths course. Without struggling I had been able to pack all my worldly possessions into the boot of my rather elderly Austin Cambridge and I waved Johannesburg goodbye and headed south. The excitement of arriving at UCT was considerable. It was always good to arrive in the Mother City and on the summer's morning that I arrived, having driven through the night, the Cape and UCT in particular seemed like something close to Utopia.

UCT's Graduate School of Business was located in Rosebank just off the Old Main Road adjacent to Baxter Hall at the bottom of the mountain and this site was about a kilometre from the Main or Upper Campus. It was a self contained rather dull "sub-campus" which was in stark contrast to the beautiful Upper Campus which contained buildings such as Jameson and Smuts Halls. Furthermore, from the Graduate School of Business sub-campus there was no need to stray for the whole duration of the programme. Indeed the work load was such that there was hardly anytime available to think about anything other than jumping through the hoops which were to be demanded of us.

The world of the Graduate School of Business did not amount to much. There was one lecture theatre and a small semi-detached library building. The library facilities were poor, but then as all the books and papers one needed for the programme were supplied it was not necessary to spend much time in the library, at least until the time for the research report, which was during the fourth term.

In an inexpensively knocked up building there was a row of minimally equipped (a blackboard, six chairs and a table) syndicate rooms. There was also a row of offices for the faculty with a student common room at the end of the row. The student common room was minimally furnished with a few easy chairs and ash trays. This was where the incoming mail was placed into pigeon holes, but perhaps more important it was where there was a fridge which held a continuous stock of beer and soft drinks. Some of us congregated there in the evenings.

There was one other separate room near the offices where tea or coffee was served on a big metal counter from enormous pots. The quality of the beverages served here was indeed inferior to the cafe in Rondebosch just down the road, but they were generally hot and wet.

Food was served for those in residence in a separate building some 20 or 30 metres away from the main area of the School.

## Old Nissen huts

Residential accommodation was offered to MBA students. There was single and married accommodation and some of the single accommodation consisted of old Nissen huts which were said to have been left over from military use. These small units consisted of four small bedrooms and a tiny shared bathroom. They were quite basic, the walls were made of some sort of light weight plasterboard and the doors were flimsy, but I guess overall they were adequate enough. Some of these small residential units were only feet away from the offices, maybe only 10 or 12 metres and they seemed uncomfortably close to the staff's working places. I was later to feel that this was embarrassing, especially when it came to the issue of the infamous telegram as the instrument of telling an MBA candidate that he or she had failed and must leave the School.

There was other accommodation arrangements made for married students adjacent to the main campus area, which was quite separate to the Nissen huts described here.

The whole land area occupied by the Graduate School of Business was probably no more than 50 metres by 50 metres. Thus it was a veritable island within the great UCT Lower Campus. And it was an island from which there was little escape, especially for those of us in the residence. Initially this small area seemed rather confining, but as time went on it was a comfort that everything was so close together. In fact I began to resent the occasions when I had to leave this small campus.

We were kept busy day and night for six days a week and even when we ventured off the premises we were never emotionally disconnected from the MBA programme. Our task masters knew how to ensure that we stayed engaged with the programme throughout.

The physical accommodation of the school was indeed minimalist, but in retrospect it appears that the Graduate School of Business was being run on a shoe string. This is rather surprising as 86 masters students would have brought a substantial amount of revenue to the university in terms of government funding.

## Pre-maths begins

On Sunday January 2 the day before the first working day of the year, as I recall, about 30 of us assembled in the lecture theatre to attend the pre-maths course. This was three weeks of wall to wall maths. This course was designed as a catch up opportunity for individuals who had not studied mathematics or used it professionally. This was a warm up event and I felt that it would allow me to ease into the business school regime.

There was no formal opening to this course as there would be to the MBA itself three weeks later. The senior faculty were away on leave.

This programme was well designed and executed in a highly effective way. The two lecturers tasked with teaching the maths connected well with the group and the general morale was high when this event ended. As well as revising some maths, these three weeks gave us an opportunity to get to know each other as well to get to know the two lecturers. This was largely achieved by consuming a quantity of the beer in the latter hours of the day. In this way we began to slowly understand some aspects of the ethos of the school.

Two relatively junior lecturers were running the maths course. One of these was an established member of Faculty while the other was an MBA graduate from the previous year. I was a little surprised that a graduate from the previous year was employed as I was conscious of the fact that we were promised that we would be "taught by the most highly skilled and experienced international faculty". Well may be the maths course was different.

## The MBA proper

On the Sunday afternoon we were all summoned into the lecture theatre. There were 86 of us. We filed into the building one by one. Standing at the door was Dave Wright (he had been one of the teachers on the maths course) and as each member of the programme passed him he inspected their dress. Arriving just in front of me one of my classmates was wearing a smart navy blue blazer with a white shirt and a tie and a pair of charcoal grey slacks. In a

low tone Dave Wright said to him, "Do not come back to this building again unless you are dressed in a business suit". I was a little
surprised at this but I had been routinely wearing a business suit
since I had started working some years ago so it hardly affected me.

The lecture theatre was a steeply banked crescent shaped affair with
four aisles which allowed the lecturers to get reasonably close to a
student if they so wished. This configuration was subsequently referred to by the MBAs as the snake pit.

When we entered the lecture theatre we found that each of us had
been pre-allocated a seat with our name displayed in front of us.
There was a pile of papers and some books already set out for us to
take. Our entrance and the taking of our place in the classroom were
conducted in a quite formal if not solemn atmosphere. We all knew
that we were embarking on a special voyage.

### The MBA ethos and the modus operandi

Once we were seated the faculty
presented themselves. Professor
Bob Boland, Professor Andre
van der Merwe, Dr Meyer Feldberg, Mr Dave Wright and Mr
Phil Reese. In addition to the
academics there were two senior
male administrators, elderly gen-
tlemen who went by the name of
Brigadier Graham and Com-
mand Mc Kraken. Bob Boland
was clearly the most senior man and the boss of the Business School.
It was Professor Boland's task to state both the ethos and the modus
operandi of UCT's Graduate School of Business which did not take
much explaining and really only consisted of a few issues. The first

and most important of this was summarised as **"Shape up or ship out"**. The first and foremost attribute of someone who was *shaping up* was that he or she would be prepared for the classroom discussions each morning. In general this meant becoming familiar with four case studies and reading perhaps as much as 50 pages of text from books and academic papers over night. But it would take several weeks for the full implications of this *Shape up or ship out* attitude to fully sink in and what it meant to those of us who wanted to survive the MBA programme.

The second issue addressed work management and the philosophy expressed by the Director was that there were never enough hours in a day for anyone to do all the things, especially all the data collection and analysis they wanted to. Business decisions were therefore always taken with incomplete information and skills had to be developed to cope with this. The only way of being able to survive the relentless demands of business was to share out work and thus it was essential that we work in groups. On the face of it this did not seem to be an unreasonable proposition. But the groups were to be used for more than work sharing. The groups were also to be a source of knowledge creation or transfer in their own right. Somehow being in or working through a group would deliver insights and understandings which could not be achieved through private study. It was never entirely clear to me how and why this should work.

There was one other important issue raised concerning the ethos of the school. Recognising the fact that there is never enough time to do everything one wants to do an important skill of a manager is to prioritise the demands on his or her time and to attend to those issues which are more important. This principle is hardly controversial but the application of this became problematic only a few weeks later.

We were told that 10% of the people in the lecture theatre (this amounted to eight or nine people) would fail and these individuals would be asked to leave i.e. "*ship out*" immediately this happened. Furthermore anyone who failed would be informed by telegram even if such a person was in residence on the grounds of the School. There would be no appeal to such a decision. We were all too naive to ask about the university's examination boards and if anyone had dared to it would probably have been a black mark against them.

We were informed that all lectures were compulsory and that if for some extraordinary reason we ever missed one we were required to apologise in writing to the lecturer and to report in order to explain ourselves to the Director of the School in person.

We were informed that the doors of the lecture theatre would be locked at the starting time each session and no-one would be admitted after the prescribed time. Coming late to a lecture was simply not an option which would be tolerated by the School.

It was made extremely clear that there was no flexibility with regards to the application of any of these rules and that we should be aware of the fact that Professor Bob Boland was for all intents and purposes the contemporary manifestation of Zeus.

The effect of this briefing was to create a high level of anxiety in the group which would stay with us at least to some extent until the end of the academic year. Whether this was good pedagogical practice was unclear at the time, but today this attitude could be accused of being bullying, which indeed it was.

This briefing did not make a good impression on me. The tone in which it was delivered was quite wrong. Also it did not seem to me that the tactics enunciated by Professor Boland were appropriate for dealing with adult men and women. The whole set up was just too draconian. Of course, no one challenged anything which was said as that would have been to invite trouble.

## The academic calendar

The academic calendar consisted of four periods of 10 weeks each, during which we were required to attend classroom sessions from 8.30 am to 1 pm with a mid-morning break. Thus there was four hours of lecturer contact per day. The rest of the day was formally unscheduled as it was necessary to prepare for the classroom sessions by private and group study. This was on the basis of only six days a week. There was no formal activity on Sundays, although during the first term there was on each second Saturday an additional activity (taking up at least part of that day) which meant that it was often necessary to work on Sundays. This Saturday work was referred to as WACS which stood for Written Analysis of Cases and will be discussed later.

The daily classroom sessions were largely devoted to the discussion of case studies and many if not most of these had come from the Harvard Business School collection. They addressed actual business situations and required both analysis and a decision as to a course of action. In the early days students tended to focus on the analysis and omit the decision. This was called analysis paralysis. But we were taught to go beyond this as the intention of the exercise was to lead to a decision being made. The case study technique as applied to business education was developed at Harvard and was regarded as a form of simulation which would give the MBA students a taste of real live business activities. Of course the use of the word simulation in this context is a malapropism as a case study will not actually create a simulation per se.

Sometimes these case studies could be 10 pages long, but on other occasions they could be 30 for 40 pages in length. It was no trivial task to read this material, to understand it, to analyse it and come to some sort of decision as to what might be done in the circumstances described by the case.

The work that was required to be completed in order to be fully prepared for the following day's classroom session could not easily be accomplished by any one individual on his or her own and thus it was necessary to work as a group to get through all the required material. At this point we had already been put into groups and for each of the forthcoming 10 week periods these groups would be changed so that we would all have an opportunity of working closely with different members of the year's intake.

The pedagogical menu consisted of four subject areas or topics for each of the first three terms and then a final term consisting of two subjects and a dissertation. A number of us were surprised that we would be allowed to fail two subjects out of the 14 subjects we had to study and be examined on. No one had heard of a degree being awarded where a candidate had actually failed subjects. There was no opportunity offered to re-write a subject and interestingly there was no mention of what might happen if an MBA student might have been ill on the day of an examination.

## Evaluation of degree candidates' performance

We were told how we would be evaluated. There would be mid-term and end of term examinations. There might or might not be impromptu tests set at any time. The importance of being able to express oneself both in writing and through verbal articulation was emphasised and thus there was a requirement to participate in class discussions for which 10% of a subject's final grade would be allocated by each subject lecturer. It was never explained how the allocation this 10% would be decided. How was the quality of the comments made by students to be assessed? How was any improvement in the comments made in the classroom to affect the mark given?

It was clear that this type of evaluation of performance had to be completely subjective and interestingly enough no one ever talked about how it might affect the outcome of an individual's term results. Could a borderline student be passed because of good class participation or could someone be failed because of silly remarks in the classroom?

We were told that there would be a prize for the best student, the Old Mutual prize as I recall. I think that there was a small amount of money attached to this accolade, but the real significance of it was the prestige of winning the prize.

Class participation played a very important role in the events of this year because by speaking out in class people were effectively airing their knowledge. Some of what was said in class was clever and showed insightful understandings of the material under review, but other comments showed a poor understanding and a lack of business experience. More will be said about this later.

**The lecturing team**

We were then introduced to the lecturing team which varied throughout the year, but which generally consisted of four members of faculty (this excludes the Director who largely took himself out of his teaching function by inventing AGL which stood for Automated Group Learning – more about this later). The small number of academics was indeed a surprise and it was the first of many to come.

In the first term of the year Dr Meyer Feldberg was to teach Marketing. Professor Andre van der Merve would teach Production Management. Mr Dave Wright and Mr Philip Reese would teach a hybrid subject called SORC which stood for Statistics, Operations Research and Computers and finally there would be no teacher for a subject called MAEC which was an acronym for Management Accounting and Control. There was no need for a teacher for this subject because Professor Boland who normally taught it had invested in a system call AGL which was an acronym for Automated Group Learning and which eliminated the need for a teacher; more about this revolutionary approach to university teaching later.

This small core faculty was supported by some visiting faculty of which, as I recall, there were four from overseas, three Americans and one from the United Kingdom. Of these four lecturers two were excellent and two were not. There were others who came to the campus to conduct parts of a course or to give an occasional invited lecture.

## The A team

It is hard to be critical of any of the individuals in the resident lecturing team. There is no doubt that Meyer Feldberg was the man on the move. Probably the second youngest member of the Faculty, he was a veritable bundle of energy and dynamism. He cut a dashing figure. He had been a national level athlete and it was said that he had swum for South Africa at some international games.

It was clear to all that he was competent in marketing. He appeared to have some considerable passion for the subject matter. He had a distinctly engaging classroom presence and there was no doubt that a

21

number of the MBA students found his lectures fully rewarding. His style was to rush around the classroom and up and down the aisles and draw as many people into the discussion as he could. Meyer knew how to do this well and he also was aware that too much movement of the teacher could be distracting as was the case with one of the other lecturers. He was intensely analytical and he taught marketing from the point of view that it was necessary to find the optimal strategy that would ensure corporate success. His genius was that he could always crack (i.e. solve) the case. Under his inspiration the class began to talk about finding the elusive case cracker which would always lead one to the right answer. A case cracker was envisaged as a checklist, which if closely followed would inevitably produce a solution and thus facilitate finding the optimal decision required to solve the challenge offered by the case study.

 Andre van der Merve on the other hand was quite different. He was a number of years older than Meyer and did not exhibit the dynamism of his younger colleague. Bald headed and a slightly round figure he was a more mature man. Although a competent academic teacher his passion for production management was not as obvious as Meyer's passion for marketing. Perhaps due to his experience there was a sense however that Professor van der Merwe was a safe pair of hands and at some level he was really concerned for the people in the class. Andre had a sense of humour and was able to tell a funny story and sometimes when he

laughed you obtained the impression that he was able to really appreciate the ridiculousness of life.

The star of the A Team was of course Professor Bobby Boland. He had the reputation of being the most gifted teacher of accounting and finance in the country and I was certainly looking forward to experiencing his technique and learning from him. It is hard to describe the level of disappointment when we were told that he would not be teaching the Management Accounting and Control course for which he had become quite famous. Bob decided that this course could be delivered through a mechanism which he called AGL. AGL involved listening to a pre-recorded lecture for maybe 10 or 15 minutes which was then immediately followed by a group discussion based around an exercise or a short case study situation. This was indeed a revolutionary approach to the teaching of accounting. The pre-recorded lecture was played by Professor Boland's secretary or personal assistant who also distributed the discussion exercise. Thus there was no qualified accounting teacher involved in the day to day running of the course. Professor Boland occasionally made an appearance, but he was not an active presence in this event.

Like the other courses offered during the first term substantial case studies also played a role in Management Accounting and Control as did three short multiple choice based books written by Professor Boland. We did sometimes learn from AGL, but it was a poor substitute for the wisdom we could have received from the master himself. In fact the reason AGL did not turn out to be a disaster was that in the groups of MBA students there were accountants who were able and prepared to explain some of the concepts which the tape recordings and worksheets addressed. Professor Boland had effectively outsourced the teaching of Management Accounting and Control to the learners themselves. This was indeed a coup for Professor

Boland, which freed him up to do other interesting things with his time.

## Other members of the academic team

Phil Reese and Dave Wright jointly ran the SORC course with the former teaching statistics and the latter taking care of the operations research and computer components of the event. Those of us who had attended the pre-maths course had already met these two relatively junior members of faculty. Phil Reese had told a group of us one night over a few bottles of beer that he was celebrating his 21st birthday that week or perhaps even that day.

In as far as he was a youthful looking man and he dressed in a modern fashion conscious way this admission had not come as a surprise. However it did seem that his presence as a member of the faculty was out of step with what had been promised in the promotion of the School because at this stage I was still anticipating the *"highly skilled and experienced international faculty"*. There also seemed to be a contradiction between the requirement that the MBA students be in their mid-twenties and have 4 years experience whilst having a young man on the faculty who had not worked before.

Phil imitated Meyers technique of rushing around the classroom and up and down the aisles, but he wasn't as skilful as Meyer and his hopping around could be distracting. He was a young man and he still had quite a lot to learn about cultivating a sophisticated class-room presence.

Dave Wright was older than Phil Reese, perhaps in his mid thirties. He had been at the School for some time and was by now an experienced teacher who was always well organised in the classroom. A fairly short man with a bald head and a rounded figure he took on the role of the Students Friend and he did this with some skill and charm. To many people he was the most solid rock and a shoulder on which one could shed a tear if it was necessary. Of course none of us ever did that. We were a hardy lot and we could take the medicine dished out to us by the School.

Personally, I always found him helpful and encouraging. He was a highly competent lecturer who did not engage in running around the classroom to the extent of the others. He primarily taught us computing. He announced early in the module that we would learn Fortran and then Basic. He was honest enough to say that Fortran was an old and relatively obsolete computer language and that when we learnt Basic we would never look at Fortran again. He would teach us Fortran in case we needed computer power and there was no Basic available. In those days user orientated computer terminals were new and UCT could not afford them. So this course was also about having computer cards punched and computer jobs queued.

## The Composition of the Class of '72

The Class of '72 was not what I expected it to be. The School had given the impression that those doing this MBA degree would be the *best young graduates who already had business experience and who were clearly cut out for senior positions in corporate life*. It had been emphasised that not everyone who applied to take this degree would be accepted. It was suggested that the refusal rate was high. It was a mark of success in its own right to have been accepted on the programme.

Of the 86 people starting this year's MBA there were about 3 or 4 who were directly out of university with no working experience. There were a few people who had working experience, but who did not have a degree. There were another 3 or 4 people who were not yet elderly, but who could no longer be referred to as young. Women were poorly represented in this class. There were four in all with one woman only joining the programme late (it seems that the door was only locked if a student was late for a classroom session) and another being thrown off the programme at the end of the first term. With regards the racial mix there was one black South African, one Chinese South African and one other South African man whose ancestors were from South Asia. At this time the Extension of University Education Act, Act 45 of 1959 was in force which prohibited racial mixing within the universities of South Africa and the School would have had to have made special application to the Minster of Education for permission to admit the three students who were not classified as whites. The country was so deeply in the grip of apartheid that this tokenism pretty well passed unnoticed and was not commented upon by anyone. In those days South Africa was a white person's world.

Among the class there were about half a dozen Chartered Accountants, one or two Cost and Management Accountants and a few others with different accounting qualifications. There were a couple of dozen engineers. There was a journalist. There was a veterinary practitioner. And there was lawyer or two. There were a number of scientists. Several people like me had social science degrees. There were some who had qualifications in the humanities. Some people had worked in personnel management, some had worked in sales and some in production and thus in a sense we were a microcosm of the world of work.

The bringing together of all these different types of people was said to be one of the great strengths of the MBA programme. Working on the MBA course material side by side with all these people from different backgrounds, professions or careers was supposed to allow their unique experiences to rub off onto one another. Exactly how this was to work was unclear and from my point of view it did not seem to work in the way that it may have been envisaged.

With regards the international dimension of the students a couple of people had come from overseas to attend this MBA. There was one man from Chile and at least one man from the UK. There were a few Rhodesians as well. But there were not enough foreigners to make a cultural impact on the group. There were other foreign students who were resident in South Africa. There was a German and a Norwegian and a few other people who were originally from the UK.

But it did not feel that the 86 of us had been selected from a larger pool of excellent applicants who had been striving to be accepted onto the programme. On one occasion I had asked Phil Reese why the School broke its rule about allowing people on the programme that did not have the business experience allegedly required. His reply was that a small number of apparently unsuitable people were admitted each year as a control group to check up on the appropriateness of the published selection requirements. I did not feel satisfied by this reply.

In general I had been quite surprised by the small number of faculty employed at the School and by the large number of students. It seemed to me that for an intensive prestigious Masters degree the student staff ratio was perhaps not what it should have been. We had been told that distinguished professors from overseas would be coming, but at this stage there was no sign of anyone who could be described in this way.

Looking at the number of people in the class who had the adequate experience to have been chosen to do this degree and who were of the right age and appeared to have top management potential it is probable that a significant number of people should not have been admitted.

## And then the year's work began

On the morning following the faculty and student get together the programme began. As mentioned before in the first term we explored Marketing, Production Management, Management Accounting and Control and SORC1 and each day two of these subjects were addressed during a two hour classroom session. During each of these sessions two case studies were discussed and sometimes there were discussions addressing the readings which we were also set for that day. Thus the menu generally consisted for 4 case studies each day.

There was a considerable volume of paper involved with this and the School's large scale photocopiers were kept busy. Case studies and readings were distributed each day by being placed in individual pigeon holes in the common room and I often cleared my incoming material a number of times a day. Just filing all the material supplied by the different course leaders was a job in its own right. The small book case in my little room rapidly began to fill with lever arch files.

The lecturer normally opened the case study by inviting a class member to introduce the story of the case and thus set the scene after which members of the class were invited to make comments or ask questions or to pose issues. Because class participation was a requirement it was normally quite easy to generate a discussion. The lecturer guided the discussion and called upon some of those class members who had not offered to make a comment. The levels of comments were interesting and revealed the business acumen of the speaker. Thus there was a reasonably wide variety of insightfulness in the comments. Occasionally a lecturer would pick on someone who was not well prepared and who gave a flaky answer. This was considered to be *"not a good thing"* as a lack of preparation was a prime indicator of *not shaping up*. We were told that black marks would be accumulated against our record. Although some lecturers were more forgiving about this than others, Bob Boland was not one of these.

This regime of four case studies and readings each day was the staple diet of the MBA, especially during the first term. The amount of effort to keep up with this was extraordinary. In the afternoons we generally worked alone in private study. I often started by reading the chapters of the text books which I was directed to read. Then I began to read the case studies and I would sometimes be able to complete this by dinner time. After dinner groups would meet and these sessions were primarily used to help each other catch up with whatever anyone had missed as well as have preliminary discussions about the main points in the case study.

## The relentless treadmill

These group meetings often went on late. There was always much to be discussed and shared and this took quite a lot of time. It was not unusual for evening group meetings to continue until close to midnight. But even when the meeting was finished the work of the day was not necessarily over. Sometimes I returned to my room and did some extra work finishing by 1 am.

On one occasion I worked through until 4 am. Nonetheless there was some time to drink and everyone had an account in the common room where beer and soft drinks were available. There were few people on this programme who worked less than an 80 hour week and some worked much more. The work was relentless. I began to feel like a galley slave. The flow of work never let up. There were always new case studies and new papers in the pigeon hole. The expression *work life balance* was not in our vocabulary in those days and it was certainly not understood by the powers that ran the Graduate School of Business.

The result of this commitment was that many of the MBA students were physically tired. By the mid-term I was beginning to feel quite exhausted, but there was no obvious way out of this treadmill as we were locked in personally to the degree as well as to the group, which had become an important part of our life.

## The Written Analysis of Cases (WAC)

In addition to the daily routine of preparing for the classroom sessions we
were set an additional hoop through
which we had to jump once every two
weeks and this was referred to as pro-
ducing a WAC. This was simply another case study, but which in this
instance had to be analysed and re-
ported on in writing. Our report had to
be typed on standardised paper supplied by the School, which was of a
special size and had particular mar-
gins.

A WAC had to be submitted on alter-
native Saturdays during the first term. There was a box into which
the WAC had to be placed. WACs were collected by a faculty member at 5 pm. It was understood that being late was not a good thing. It
was said that a student would lose a grade level for every minute he
or she was late. As a result of this draconian policy, as far as I am
aware, no one was ever late. It was also said that a grade level would
be lost for every typographical or spelling error made in the document. If any of the text touched the margin a grade would be similarly lost.

Virtually no one aspiring to a management position could type in
those days. In fact being able to type was seen as a near deviant be-

haviour for managers until into the 1990s.The School provided a list of approved typists. These women lived either in Rondebosh itself or in adjacent areas. Therefore it was necessary to go to their home to have the WAC typed. A hand written copy was produced and taken to the typist, usually on the Thursday night. This allowed time to return on the Friday to check the typed document. If it was perfect it was then collected. If not corrections had to be made and a second trip to the typist made the following day.

This added an additional layer of work and anxiety to the MBA process.

## Impromptu tests and other work challenges

We had been told that there would be impromptu tests and work assignments which could be sprung on us at any time. As it turned out there was not really any time for this type of test as our daily schedule was so busy already. However one such test did take place when we arrived in the classroom at 8.30 one morning. A so called blue book was distributed and we were instructed to write on a topic covered during the previous week. This only happened once and thus its impact on the programme was hardly felt. Similarly one evening while we were getting going with our group work an additional assignment was distributed and we were required to produce an answer immediately, i.e. that evening. This was in addition to the normal workload.

My impression was that impromptu tests and assignments meant additional grading for the staff and that was not popular with them either and thus it did not become a feature of the programme.

## Conversing with Zeus

During the first term we did not see Bob Boland on the campus much. It was rumoured that he was in Australia selling his AGL technique to a big oil company. But one afternoon towards the middle of the term I was in the room in which the tea was served when Bob Boland arrived. I was having a quiet cup of tea and I didn't want to be engaged in conversation by anyone. He walked up to me and asked how I was getting on. I replied that I was alright but I was tired from the intensity of the work required. I went one step further and said that I did not think that anyone could sustain performance under the pressure we were being put through. I said that it was impossible to work 80 hour weeks on a continual basis.

## Pressure is always only in the mind

Boland did not take well to these comments and he replied sharply, *"Who says that?"* I was of course completely out of my depth. I had no supporting evidence that 80 hour weeks would present anyone with a problem. It was time for me to shut up. Boland went on to say that, *"Pressure is always only in the mind. We impose pressure upon ourselves. If you want to, you can take the afternoon off and sleep or perhaps go to the cinema. Your life is your own do with it want you like"*. I was not really able to make sense of Boland's comments.

## Identify what is really important

Around about the same time I had another encounter with Boland which was not entirely pleasant. On one occasion, as well as setting case studies the MAEC course required MBA students to undertake a large bookkeeping exercise. We were presented with 50 or 60 financial transactions and asked to enter them into a set of accounts and then to draw up a trial balance, income statement and a balance sheet. Out of character with all the other tasks we were set during the MBA year, this rather simple and mechanistic bookkeeping exercise was really of little value to anyone. Perhaps it was required so that the drudgery of manual accounting would be made apparent.

The ins and outs of double entry bookkeeping was quite difficult for many people on the programme who had not been drilled in the difference between a debit and a credit. As I had worked as an accountant this type of exercise was second nature to me and I found myself helping a number of people with their exercise. Before I knew what had happened I found that I had run out of time to complete this task. I then remembered the point made by Boland during our inaugural lecture. The professor had said that because of the lack of time we all had to live with, it was crucial to identify what was really important and to concentrate on those issues. I then worked out that it had been important for me to help people with the bookkeeping exercise and that it was not necessary for me to do it myself. Consequently I did not submit this piece of work.

A couple of days later I received a note in my pigeon hole that I should report to the Directors Office. It did not immediately occur to me what might be the cause of this, but it was unusual enough for me to attend to the matter immediately.

I therefore presented myself to the professor's secretary. On entering his office I was asked, *"Why have you not completed the assignment this week?"* *"I didn't have the time to do it"*, I said. He looked at me as though I had committed the greatest heresy possible. *"I spent a lot of time helping others with that bookkeeping problem and the time just escaped me. And as I have worked with accounts for a number of years that exercise had no value to me. I was following your advice of doing what is important"*. *"So you are a Chartered Accountant"*, he asked. *"No. I am not"*, I replied. *"You have a Cost and Management Accounting qualification then?"* he asked. *"No. I have no accounting qualification. I would describe myself as an economist, but I have worked as an accountant for a number of years and I can present accounts at any level. I have also been a part-time lecturer in accounting at the Durban Technical College"*.

Not being prepared to take me at face value the professor then quizzed me about accounting procedures. He set me a number of scenarios and asked me how they should be treated from an accounting point of view.

Having satisfied him that I knew accounting I was dismissed from his office. Zeus had spoken to me twice, but was I blessed or cursed?

I certainly could not tell. But I did learn that I should have identified that the work set by the Director was probably the most important of all the assignments.

## Social events

Besides socialising over a bottle of beer in the common room late at night there were several social events held by the class. There was a beach party. There were some barbeques and other outings.

I recall an especially excessive evening at a wine estate called Backsberg. In those days it was not socially unacceptable to drink and then drive. Most of us were young and getting some time away from the School was special.

The social life must have been much better than I thought it was as the time as several people have now told me that this was the best part of the programme from their point of view.

It is important to say that I did make a few friends during that year and that these friendships have been long term and important to me.

## Mid-term exams

In order to keep the pressure at the appropriate level we were faced with yet another obstacle which was the mid-term exams. There was no practical need for mid-term exams as the term was only 10 weeks long. It just introduced another reason for anxiety. It was not perfectly clear as to the percentage of the final marks that were allocated to these exams. We knew that 10% was for class participation, but how the mid-term and final examinations marks were split was not clear.

These exams like all other ones we faced during the year were open book. This meant that most of us carried a large pile of books and placed them around us as we wrote our answers to the exam questions. These exams were, as one would have expected, based on case studies.

The results were provided quickly enough. I do not recall learning anything from the mid-term exam process.

## The second half of the first term

In the second half of the first term a number of thoughts occurred to me about the MBA programme. First of all, few if any of the case studies had any relevance to me. The case studies in all the subjects were descriptions of American organisations that were mostly facing issues and problems which did not exist in South Africa. I often wondered what some company located in the mid-west of the USA that employed 5,000 people making some sort of widget for the aerospace industry had to do with anything I was likely to encounter in my career. The environments were different. The culture was different. The people were different. I began to wonder why American management practices were believed to be so important to aspirant South African managers. Thinking more carefully about this there were virtually no issues in common between any of these organisations and those that we found in South Africa. It is true to say that come of the companies studied had branches in South Africa so the names were known to us. But the issues in these companies were those which concerned the Head Office and not the branch at the end of Africa.

It was in the second half of the first term that I began to wonder if I might not have made the right decision in coming to do an MBA at UCT.

## The routine grinds on and on

By the second half of the first term we were well and truly mesmerised by the punishing routine. There was no time for anything else but the daily grind of preparing for the classroom session the following morning and the writing of the WAC. We had to put the rest of our lives on hold. In general Saturday night was the only time one was able to get away from the place and even then the work load was always on one's mind. This did not seem to have been much of a problem for the 86 people in this year's intake. There was actually very little grumbling. It was a ridiculous regime and it is surprising that it was so completely accepted.

There were rumours that in previous years the work commitment had caused marital problems for some of the students. It was said that there had been divorces but the class of 1972 appeared to not have been bothered by this. There was some effort made to offer some sort of entertainment to some of the wives. I understand that Andre van der Merwe conducted cooking classes in the evening at one point in order to entertain the wives.

## Final exams at the end of the first term

In the 10th week we wrote final exams in the four subjects. Once again these consisted of case studies. Using case studies for examination purposes can be seen as problematic due to the different speeds at which people read. This is especially true when relatively long case studies are used. This was to become an important issue at the end of the second term when a scandal about the examinations broke out. Professor Boland and his team showed no concern about the length of case studies in examinations.

Once again the exams were open book and we brought our books and notes with us. The interesting thing about open book examinations is that there is seldom if ever any opportunity to refer to these books and papers. The examination is such (and this especially applies to a case study examination) that if one needs to refer to a book than it is unlikely that there is any prospect of passing the exam. In the 14 exams I wrote while at the Graduate School of Business I did not obtain any information from any of the books I religiously brought with me to the examinations. But it did feel good to have my books at my feet.

## Intellectual achievement at the end of the first term

It is difficult to decide how the intellectual or the academic achievements of the group of people should be described at the end of the first term. The four topics we had studied were all at the introductory level. There was no depth in any of it and I guess one of the lessons that this programme taught was that one could obtain a considerable and useful understanding without having to study a subject in depth. Those who came to the MBA from a professional engineering background would probably have found new things to learn in Management Accounting and Control and maybe marketing. Those who qualified as accountants through the articles route only may well have gained something from the other three subjects. Those who had no working experience probably benefited the most from the programme as well as the vet and the journalist.

The production management module was perhaps especially light weight. I had certainly covered all the material in a first year industrial management course I had done several years before. In order to compensate for this a bit Andre van der Merwe organised a visit to a factory. We were taken to a cigarette factory in Paarl. Factory visits seemed to me to be a bit out of place, but it was interesting to see how it was possible to make hundreds of thousands of cigarettes a day or maybe it was hundreds of thousands of cigarettes an hour. However it was clear that this was a break from the School rather than an integrated part of the programme.

For those with a general business background there wasn't much new by way of ideas or concepts on offer as all the material addressed so far would have been covered in a bachelor of commerce degree. The claim that *"This degree was based on the latest business and pedagogical thinking and practices from Harvard University in the USA"* was delivered in that Harvard Business Review articles were supplied from time to time and that Harvard case studies had been used in the classroom sessions. We are yet to experience *"the most highly skilled and experienced international faculty"*.

There is one other interesting comment to be made. Despite the pre-maths course and the fact that SORC was taught competently there were those in the class who were not comfortable with numerical analysis. In order to compensate for this each technique we were taught was always accompanied by a list of *non-quantitative factors that should be taken into account.* On one entertaining occasion a

member of the class said, "I can't calculate a single statistic, I can't calculate a NPV, I can't produce any linear programming equations but I can give you all the *non-quantitative factors* involved.

## The results of the exams

We were given a week's break after the first 10 weeks of the MBA. Of course for those of us who had enrolled for the pre-maths we had been working intensively for 13 weeks. Anyway many of us escaped from the Graduate School of Business for that week and came back relatively refreshed. But not all of us returned.

The exams resulted in four people being asked to leave. In terms of the rules which said that one could fail two subjects and still obtain an MBA, this meant that four people had failed at least three of the four subjects written at the end of the first term. This suggests a failure in either candidate selection or in support for the learning process or both. But at the time no comment was made.

What was truly remarkable about this was the fact that the School was able to have the scripts marked and the marks moderated and the results placed before a higher degrees examination board for confirmation within a week.

There were two aspects of the failures which bothered me. One of the men who were failed lived in the residence adjacent to the Nissen Hut I lived in. His Nissen Hut was one of the closest to the Director's

Office, being between 10 and 12 metres away. I felt uncomfortable about the system which involved the Director or one of his under-lings sending a telegram to someone who was 10 or 12 metres away. It seemed to me to indicate a possible lack of moral fortitude on the part of the Director. A face to face review with the failed student and an opportunity to say farewell seemed to me more appropriate than a telegram.

Secondly there was the matter of the woman student who failed at the end of the first term. During one of the classroom sessions this female student made a markedly negative comment about the way the School was being run. At the time it struck me that she was cou-rageous as it was quite plain that the Director was not interested in obtaining any negative feedback. This woman's class participation wasn't poor and I wondered how she managed to fluff her exams to such an extent that she was kicked out. Of course strange things hap-pen in examinations and even the brightest of students have been known to make a complete mess when the pressure is really on. There is no doubt that we all were feeling the pressure at this stage of the degree.

In addition to the 4 people being removed from the programme a number of others had failed one subject and some may even have failed two. With 4 people having been despatched it meant that the School was really serious about failing people and that there were probably 4 or 5 others to be thrown out before the end of the year.

**The second term**

We were now faced with four new subjects which were Finance, Human Relations and Organisation, SORC 2 and Economics. The Finance was to be taught by Professor Bob Boland, but of course he was busy and he wasn't able to do all of it. Thus he had a helper who ran a number of his classes for him. This was the domain of Dr

Meyer Feldberg and many members of the class welcomed the idea of having him teach us again. SORC 2 was taught by Dave Wright who had some help from a visiting professor from overseas, the USA to be precise. And Economics was taught by an outsider, who as I recall worked in some organisation in Cape Town.

Meyer Feldberg taught Human Relations and Organisation with the same gusto as he had conducted the marketing module the term before. It was case study after case study, but now having lived through a couple of hundred case study sessions they did not seem to be quite so formidable. But preparing for them was still a labour intensive business.

The SORC 2 course featured Dave Wright on how maths could be used to optimise procedures in business. It was a different take on SORC and Dave had help from a POSH American professor. We settled into a routine of discussing the techniques and their strengths and weaknesses as much as actually using them.

The Economics module attempted to cover all the topics I had studied during my three year Economics major. It was interesting to see just how superficially this subject could be taught and how the MBA students were able to pick up the language of Economics without any real understanding of the issues which lay behind the words.

We were then offered the services of Professor Boland to teach Finance. It was somewhat of a letdown. Here was the man who had been described as the most gifted teacher in South Africa and the impression he made when he eventually taught us was quite minimal. It was said in muted tones that he was really a Management Accounting man and that Finance was not really his strong suit. But even if this were true he had a credibility deficit with regards to his style. He did not bring the energy level to his classroom performance that Meyer Feldberg did. However we did have the opportunity to see

Professor Boland's vindictiveness. On one occasion he identified a person who had not prepared the case study for that morning. When the student was not able to answer the question about the case Boland pressed him until the student admitted he had not read the case. Boland went on to another class member to discuss the point. But after a few minutes Boland went back the miscreant who had not properly prepared for the class and started to ask him questions again. One more time the unhappy student had to admit that he wasn't prepared. And Boland then moved on only to come back to this student again and rub in the fact he had not been prepared. I felt embarrassed by this unnecessary attempt to shame the student in this way.

Boland was away from the campus just as much in the second term as he had been in the first and thus he was never really part of the programme.

## New groups

In order to ensure that everyone had the opportunity of getting to know everyone else new groups were established each term. Our names were shuffled and we were now faced with getting to know new people and learning how to work with them. This was another challenge which seemed to work better in some cases than in others. I do not recall the names of all the members of my second group but I do recall two individuals and one unfortunate incident. The case study regime did not work quite as well for Economics as it did for the other subjects and thus we had other work to prepare.

One of the tasks for economics was to produce a considerable report on some topic of national and international importance. The report was to be worth 10% of our final marks. This task required us to divide the work up among the six of us. One of the women students was our chairperson or leader for this project and she coordinated the project. In due course the work was completed by all the individuals concerned and handed in and compiled into the final report and then submitted. A couple of weeks later we were informed that we were awarded zero. One section of the report was determined to be an exact copy of material from another published source and thus we were guilty of plagiarism.

There was nothing we could do about this. We were expected to have collective responsibility. There was no way in which we could have all read the full report. It was unreasonable for us to have expected our chairperson to have read the whole thing either.

The loss of the marks did not matter to me as it would not affect whether or not I passed this subject in which I already a degree. But our chairperson was a potential prize winner and the marks were thus probably more important to her.

## The Big Shock

A few weeks into the second term we had a big shock. Professor Bob Boland was no longer Director of the Graduate Business School. The Directorship was transferred to Meyer Feldberg who was now Professor Meyer Feldberg. At the same time we were told that Professor Andre van der Merwe had left UCT was now employed at Stellenbosch Business School.

I guess quite a lot of people were surprised if not shocked by this turn of events. However Bob Boland was hardly ever around in the months leading up to this change in leadership and so it was hard to see how this change could make all that difference. None of us had any idea why Bob resigned this post, but the rumour which ran rife around the School was that when he had been in Australia selling AGL the Dean or the Vice-Chancellor or both discovered that he was out of the country during term time without the requisite permissions and ordered him back. The rumours said that either he didn't come back or he came back reluctantly and this produced the circumstances of his resignation. It was generally believed that losing the Directorship did not bother Bob Boland one little bit as it gave him even more time to develop AGL. It was said that he went on to create AGL products to teach a host of other subjects and used this idea of impersonal learning all over the word.

But Bob Boland had the manner, he had the gravitas and he had the looks of a Director of an important Business School. Meyer Feldberg looked like a champion swimmer which indeed he was.

The loss of Andre van der Merwe was the double whammy. Andre had been more committed to the School as least in as far as he had spent more time there that year and was more engaged with the students. So his loss was more directly felt. None of us were privy to why he moved on to Stellenbosh University, but the rumours were that he had expected to be Bob's successor. He had not been scheduled to teach in the second term so this did not directly affect us and he was kind enough to agree to become a visiting professor at the UCT School for the third term during which he taught Advanced Finance as an elective to those who wanted to follow this course.

## The big grind

The work ground on and on. We were kept working full time but perhaps not quite for 80 hour weeks anymore. At least the WACs were over. The pressure varied a bit depending on the length of the case studies on a particular night. On one occasion we had a particularly large work load and I worked very late. The following morning I was considerably more tired than usual and by the tea break I decided that I should return to my room and take a 10 minute cat nap. This was the first and only time I ever did this. I fell into a deep sleep and I work up at 12.30. This meant that I had been absent from a lecture. This absence was an unusual occurrence and it had only been done a couple of times in total in the previous term and a half.

I knew the required procedure. I quickly wrote a note of apology to Dave Wright whose session I had missed and I handed it in to the School secretary and I made an appointment to see the Director.

That afternoon I was ushered into Professor Feldberg's office. He was sitting at his desk writing as I enter the officer. Without looking up at me he said, *"So what do you want?"* *"I have come to apologise for missing a classroom session"*, I said. *"Why were you not there?"* he asked. I felt a complete idiot to have to say, *"I was very tired and I fell asleep during the tea break and woke up after the session had begun"*. *"Don't do it again"*, were his final words. I had now been interviewed by the next generation of Zeus.

## A pleasant moment

In the midst of the grind of the second term I personally had a pleasant moment. One afternoon as I sat at my desk there was a knock on my door. I called out, *"Come in"*, and to my surprise there was one of my classmates who had come to ask me a favour. *"I am getting married in a couple of days and I wonder if you would be kind enough to be my best man?"* What a surprise and what a pleasant one to boot. I didn't know this person well, but we had conversed a few times over tea and at lunch time. *"I am honoured to be asked and it would be a pleasure to be part of your celebrations"*. So on the following Saturday morning a small group of us went to Cape Town

Magistrates Court where we were ushered into the registrar's office. The bride and groom signed the book and I and another signed as witnesses. This process took less than a couple of minutes. There was absolutely nothing to the ceremony (i.e. no vows) besides the formality of signing the documents.

We piled into a car and went back to Baxter Hall, which was the woman's residence where his bride was living. We had tea and cake with the warden and a few other invited guests. An hour or so later I was back working in my room and my classmate was taking a 2 day honeymoon.

## Mid-term exams again

Mid-term exams were another distraction which brought with them their own special anxiety, but this time these exams were nothing special.

In general the routine and the endless slog carried us through the rest of the 10 weeks and we faced the final exams like old hands at this game.

## Escaping from the School

By the middle of the second term it was clear to me that there were so many short comings in the way the School was being run that I may have made a mistake in signing up for this programme. I wrote a few pages outlining all my complaints. I invited the class president to come to my room to discuss them. When I started reading my script I was overwhelmed with a feeling of how stupid I had been to take on this degree without performing the requisite research that would have alerted me to the draconian regime and I wasn't able to finish reading what I had written.

It also occurred to me clearly that day that I could leave the School as everyone would simply believe that I wasn't up to the standard required to obtain this fabulous degree. I was truly boxed in.

## Intellectual achievement at the end of the second term

We had covered a lot of material. I had purchased many lever arch files in which I had packed endless case studies and readings. I had come to realise that the case study method had several limitations. I was sceptical about the value of focusing so intently on American business scenarios. I did realise that there were very few South African case studies available and when we encountered them in term three we didn't like them much. The School had a tendency to overwhelm us with readings from journals including the Harvard Business Review, which were by and large of little value.

## Apartheid, Protest and UCT

On June 2 of this year the South African police broke up a peaceful student demonstration which was being held on the steps of the Anglican Cathedral in Cape Town. Several hundred UCT students had gathered for a protest against the general unfairness of apartheid. When the students refused to disperse the police decided to baton charge them. This was the first time that such outright violence had been used so publicly against white students. Furthermore this violence was at least to some extent perpetrated on church property. When some of the students retreated into the Cathedral they were followed by police who dragged them out and threw them to the ground. Some 50 students were hurt or arrested in the fracas which followed. Left wing political elements in South Africa found this event very offensive. The police action was given the full support of the Prime Minister, Mr JB Vorster.

There were various meetings at the University concerning this matter, one of which was held at the School. The issue raised was to do with whether lectures would be cancelled to allow those members of the class who so wished, the opportunity to attend another protest meeting at the Cathedral following the police brutality. The School management decided that this decision should be left up to the MBA class itself.

By this stage the class that been psyched up to believe that every single moment of contact with the faculty was precious and should under no circumstances be missed. So the question was How could we countenance the loss of contact time with the faculty in order to go down town to an undergraduate orientated protest meeting? The School meeting to discuss this issue was chaired by Meyer Feldberg and it appeared to me that he wanted us to show our solidarity and sympathy with the rest of the University who strongly objected to what had happened and that he was supporting the next protest. But most of the 80 odd people in the room were now intensely orientated to their own personal objectives and were not necessarily interested in the greater University of Cape Town position.

I do not recall the exact outcome of this School meeting except that I was uncomfortable that the class had not been more offended by the police action. Some of us attended the protest meeting at the Cathedral the following day, when several thousand people turned out and all the streets around the cathedral were packed with protesters. On this occasion there was no baton charge but the police let off tear gas which made the crowd disperse.

So with a whiff of tear gas I made my way back to the School where some of us talked about what would happen after the revolution.

## The third term

We had been given a three week break and some of us took ourselves as far from the Graduate School of Business as possible. I had driven to Johannesburg with a classmate in a clapped out old car and we had found ourselves stranded in Beaufort West where we ended up sleeping on a mattress in a store room in the local police station.

## The T- Groups

But now we were back and ready to face whatever the School had to throw at us and indeed there was a new hoop through which we had to jump. This was referred to as T-Groups or sensitivity training. We were required to spend 5 days in larger groups than usual, about 12 people as I recall, exploring each other's foibles. This was something completely different. When not involved in exercises we sat in a big circle most of the time and we talk to each other. We did have a guide who spent some of the time with us.

The first exercise had us stand in a tight circle almost shoulder to shoulder. Then one of us moved into the middle of the circle facing the others. Standing face to face only 6 inches between our noses (we were told to stand really close to the person in front of you) the person in the circle was supposed to tell the person opposite him or her exactly what he or she really felt about that person.

There were several variations on this type of exploration of us and the other members of the group.

A different exercise required each member of the group to write down in disguised handwriting his or her darkest fear and place them in a box. These were then discussed openly by the group. There were more physical exercises, which involved jumping into groups of people who were trying to keep you out and also trying to escape from people who were trying to hold you in a particular location.

There was one particular insightful exercise where everyone was asked to slowly lean backwards to a point where they would fall on their back. It was not intended that anyone should hit the ground as the other members of the group were standing by to catch the person concerned. I did not willingly participant in this exercise and when I did it was an eerie feeling to have placed this amount of trust in the people in my group. However there were others who were simply not able to bring themselves to this level of trust which they felt to be out of place on an MBA programme and they refused to play this game.

It seemed that the purpose of the T-Group week was to have people get to know each other better and to build up a level of trust. It is extremely difficult to do this properly and there are risks involved when people drop their natural guard. This cannot be achieved without continuous expert guidance and this was not adequately provided. Thus in a sense the potential of this week was missed.

It is also ironical that an event which addressed trust in this way was incorporated into an environment where the ethos was so draconian and unsympathetic to the learner. By this stage I certainly did not trust the School in any commonly understood sense of the word.

Nonetheless some of us took really well to those sessions. Many were really quite indifferent. They were just another hoop UCT wanted us to jump through. But a few people found the activities of the T-Groups difficult and this then appeared to create some degree of emotional distress.

There is no question that the T-group week was interesting although it probably could have been conducted over two days instead of a week. But the question with which I was left after this experience was *How did it fit into a Masters degree from UCT?* No one was ever able to give me a satisfactory answer to this question.

## A computerised business game

At this time a business game was played. An itinerant American professor turned up with a large computer program which was run on the university mainframe and we were engaged in making many different decisions covering most aspects of a business in order to maximise the simulated profit. Some people appeared to like this quite a lot. But to me it did not seem to be well integrated into any other aspect of the MBA programme and was thus more of a distraction than anything else.

## The second term exam results

The results of the second term exams were published and as I recall it, two or maybe it was three more people were kicked off the programme making it six or seven people removed in total. This was a bit like the ray gun in the science fiction movies were someone is vaporised. Our erstwhile classmates were found wanting. They were sent the telegram and they simply just disappeared. But this time there was a problem with the rest of the exam results.

Because of class participation it was apparent who were the really bright hard working individuals in the class. This was evident due to the quality of the comments which were made during the class discussions. It was clear who was in contention for the top of the class Old Mutual Prize. As a result of the first term exams one of the less accomplished members of the class had obtained very high marks and was ranked in

the top three or the top five. Many of us were surprised by this, but it was accepted as beginners luck. When the same thing happened at the end of the second term the explanation of beginners luck began to be questioned. I am not quite sure what steps were actually taken but an enquiry was initiated. A few days later it was said that the student in question had been able to see the examination papers in advance. But the papers had not been supplied by the faculty or by the administration staff.

The problem was a bit more endemic than that. It was said that the School had used the same case studies in examinations in previous years. The student in question had friends who had completed the MBA the year before and had access to those exam papers. Getting access to these papers was of course in the eyes of the School nothing more than good research practice.

It was really hard to believe that UCT would have allowed this to have happened. It seemed to me to be hardly believable that this could have happened in a university with the reputation and standing of UCT. There also seemed to be no consequences associated with this unfortunate behaviour.

For me one of the interesting issues related to this but never addressed, was the use of case studies in examinations. By using case studies one gives a great advantage to the fast reader. Fast reading does not indicate any special intellectual gift, but it gives more time for writing and in a time restricted exam situation this is critical to the results which can be achieved.

## Visiting faculty and others

The third term involved more visiting faculty, a number of whom were quite disappointing. As mentioned above the business game was administered by an American professor. We had another American who was an expert on international commodity markets who introduced us to the wonders of the pork belly market and also about how the market could be cornered. From the home front we also had a man from UNISA who came to teach Business Policy. Many business schools use visiting faculty, who come to teach for anything from a few hours to a few months. Because of the beauty of the Cape UCT does not have difficulty in finding visiting faculty. But the quality of visiting faculty can be quite variable.

From the home team we had Dave Wright taking us for Management Information Systems and we were offered a choice from a few so called elective courses. The choice was some variation on operations research, consumer behaviour and advanced finance. I chose advanced finance because it was being taught by Andre van der Merwe and I had enjoyed my contact with him during the production management module. I was also interested to see how Andre would teach advanced finance as I was under the impression that he had no experience in this field of study at all.

## The pork belly man

The first international visiting professor to take a course was an expert in the field of commodity trading. This was a new area to many of us and some of us were indeed fascinated to learn that you could buy futures in pork bellies. For those of us interested in pursuing a career in this field he would have been useful, but for many us his subject seemed to be of relatively minor interest.

He was supposed to be an international star – one of these high pow-ered lecturers who would be bringing the latest business thinking to South Africa. At one point he talked about the use of mathematics in market modelling and in so doing he said, "Have you guys done cal-culus?" I realised that he may not have been aware that he was speaking to a class of graduates. He clearly had not been told about the pre-maths course or about what was covered in SORC.

## The business policy man

The School brought down to Cape Town from Pretoria a distinguished professor from UNISA to run the busi-ness policy course. He held a senior position in UNISA and he was sold to us as being an authority on all aspects of business policy. Unfortunately he did not make a good impression from the start. As UNISA was then a corre-spondence university (today it is re-ferred to as a distance or e-Learning university) he was not an accom-plished lecturer. He would have done very little teaching at UNISA and he would probably not have had much experience in front of groups of execu-tives. He may well have had much to teach us, but he was not able to work with the culture of the School and his style was resented. He was also a disappointment in another way. Until his arrival we had virtually no South African case studies and this was beginning to be noticed by some of us. With the arrival

of the Professor from UNISA we were informed that he had written a number of cases about South African business. This was indeed true. The cases he had written were mostly about South African parastatals such as ISCOR and ESCOM. They were long case studies which addressed some of the complex issues involved in these important economic sectors. But there was little interest in the MBA students about these subjects which were not deemed as being central to the business scene in South Africa.

## Rescued by Taylor

I do not know exactly how this was brought about, but a complaint was raised about how this module was proceeding and Professor UNISA was removed. This may have been a little unfair but he had not gone down well with the class. The man who replaced him was Professor Bernard Taylor from Henley Management College in the United Kingdom. Bernard Taylor was either the leading authority or at least one of the leading authorities on Corporate Strategy in the United Kingdom and he was an accomplished lecturer. Although he did not have South African case studies he did bring some non-American cases with him.

Professor Taylor spent much of his time at Henley Management College teaching senior executives as this was the main business of that institution. He therefore had a style which matched what we were now expecting. He used great coloured slides and I recall being impressed with how well he was prepared for his lecture session.

His presence brought a refreshing new mind to the School's faculty and was appreciated by most of us.

## The local team

In 1972 Management Information Systems was a new subject and therefore there was not much published research on the subject and what there was tended to be rather elementary. Dave Wright provided us with some insights into the trials and tribulations that could be experienced when computers were purchased without adequate planning and especially without an appropriate level of commitment from top management.

Andre van der Merwe conducted a remarkable advanced finance course. He managed to keep the small group who did it interested and occupied. One of Andre's hallmark techniques was to tell interesting stories about the subject he was teaching in order to illustrate issues and also to amuse his audience. The one story which remains with me from this course was on the issue of mergers and acquisitions. As a young graduate in the late 1950's, so his story went, Andre had been the executive personal assistant to a rather famous South African entrepreneur who I will call Jan. Jan had many businesses, one of which he wanted to sell. To this end Andre had spent many weeks conducting a thorough analysis of all aspects of the business in order to scientifically establish its value. It was decided that the value of the business was about £300,000. In those days South Africa used the pound as the unit of currency. An interested party contacted Jan and asked for a meeting to discuss the possible purchase of the business.

Andre and Jan met the prospective purchasers of the business across the table in the boardroom. Jan opened the discussion with the question, *"Well how much would you offer us for the business?"* The reply which came through was, *"We have done our homework and we have established that we could not justify paying more than £700,000 for this business"*. *"That price is out of the question"*, said Jan. *"I would not be prepared to take less than a million pounds for it!"* An hour later Jan and the purchaser shook hands on a price of £850,000.

After the meeting was finished and when Jan and Andre were on their own Andre asked, *"What was going on in that negotiation? Had we not decided that we would take £300,000?"* Jan's reply was, *"If those fools thought that the business could have been worth £700,000 then they had no idea what they were doing and it was obvious to me that I could get an even higher price than they initially offered. In actual fact it is poor business practice to ever accept the opening offer!"*

This was sound advice indeed.

### New groups and work loads

Once again we had new groups with which to work. However the work load was now lightened. The 80 hour weeks were over. It was still necessary to be in the classroom on time, to wear a business suit and to be prepared for discussions, but we were now less concerned about the outcome of the year. After all six or seven people had been eliminated from the programme and that meant that if they were going to throw eight or nine people off in total only another one or two were to be axed. And by now there were several people with two failed subjects and so they were in the firing line. Although for most of us the probability of being thrown out had now been significantly reduced, one further person was axed at the end of the third term.

In general we could see the end in sight and that gave encouragement to many of us. But it was still a grind to complete all the work that we were presented.

The presence of Professor Boland was not noticeable on the campus and we did not see all that much of Professor Feldberg who was not teaching that term.

### Excreta tauri cerebrum vincit

Class participation was something that a number of us were suspicious of. It was required by the School probably only for the reason of keeping classroom sessions going. A classroom session had to last the requisite amount of time and could not be allowed to fizzle out.

A number of people in the class liked to speak and sometimes they were wordier than they should have been. In recognition of this the Tri-Beta Fraternity was established. The motto of this fraternity was Excreta tauri cerebrum vincit and this could be translated as *the manure of the bull conquers the brain.* The meaning of the tri-beta will be obvious to anyone who reflects on it for a moment. About 10 members of the class were elected to this Fraternity each year. I do not recall how they were nominated or how a vote was taken. A special tie was presented to those who were so elected and I should say that this is the only souvenir of my MBA I have retained.

## Intellectual achievement at the end of the third term

We had now been exposed to a few of these *"highly skilled and experienced international faculty"* and it was clear that they were a mixed bunch. Although the Pork Belly Man did not do much for many of us, Bernard Taylor did. This term delivered the message that on the whole our local team were not bad.

I also came to realise that finishing this MBA programme would be a personal achievement for me, irrespective of any intellectual development I might experience.

## Final exams at the end of the third term

The exams came and went without much incident except for the person who was thrown off the programme. There was some comment made in hushed tones that it was unfair to boot someone off the course so late in the year. The system at the School should have identified his weakness earlier in the year and got rid of him then. But nothing came of this.

## The fourth term

The atmosphere had now changed considerably. This term was quite different to anything else we had been put through.

There had been a problem at the School since its inauguration related to the number of people who actually graduated with the degree each year. It appeared that the School was so successful in helping to place those who had done the programme at the end of the course that a material number of people had not completed all the requirements for the degree

to be awarded by UCT. It was certainly interesting to learn that in the early years the real emphasis of the School was on facilitating students to obtain high paid high visibility jobs and not necessarily on graduation.

The Masters degree at UCT required a research element. At the School this was called the research report and was also sometimes referred to as a dissertation. Up until this time the university had been relaxed about waiting for these research reports, but it had now decided to impose a deadline.

This problem with the research reports caused the School to rethink its policy and in our year we were strongly encouraged to complete the research report immediately and to thus graduate in the same year. To facilitate this we had only two subjects to cope with during the fourth term, but we were also expected to finish the research report as well. A number of us took up this challenge and passed the two exams and submitted a satisfactory research report and graduated in mid-December.

## The research report

The research report experience was seen as an adjunct to the main event which was now rapidly coming to a close. There was little advice given as to how this should be done. A supervisor was allocated, but it was fairly clear that the research report was to be completed quickly.

To this end I undertook a market survey using a consumer panel and produced an entirely undistinguished piece of work. But it was on time. The topic I studied was Airline Marketing as I had a particular interest in the airline industry and I managed to present it to South African Airways. As a result of this I was immediately made a firm job offer. However due to South African Airways bureaucracy they could only recruit me, having obtained a masters degree, at a salary which was lower than the one I had before resigning to embark on the MBA. I offered to take the job if they could match my pre-MBA salary, but they were totally inflexible and so I declined this opportunity.

Some people argue that it is the research report which allows an educational event like this MBA to be regarded as a masters degree. This report is supposed to engage the degree candidate at a level beyond that which would be achieved for a bachelors degree. There was little evidence of this at the School.

## Job interviews

From early in this term prospective employers began to visit the campus and interview members of the class. We were asked to prepare résumés for this purpose.

It appeared that the employers were mostly interested in the engineers and the accountants. An MBA on top of an engineering qualification was seen as a particularly attractive combination. The combined knowledge of technology and business was a formula to obtain a good job. Accountants also seemed to have no trouble in finding great openings. As the MBA had opened their horizons they were now seen to be more rounded. With regards to everyone else my impression was that most people had some interest shown in them by an employer or two. In my case I had two job suggestions. One of the large food producers told me

that I would be suitable to apply for the deputy managership of one of their mushroom factories where there was a vacancy.

I declined to follow this through. I was told by the large firm of in-solvency administrators in Cape Town that I had the right qualifications to join them. However before formally applying for a position they asked me to think carefully about the fact that I might be asked to go with a bailiff on Christmas eve and repossess a person's assets or even their home. When I reflected on this I realised that this type of work was not for me. I was offered and took up a short term consulting position with a small firm. But after the MBA I wanted to experience corporate life in a large multinational and so I remained with this small firm for a short period before setting out for Johannesburg to seek my fortune or rather my future.

## Intellectual achievement at the end of the fourth term

Every case study is uniquely different. Each has its own story, its own character and its own outcome. There is no denying that much can be learnt from case studies. It is sometimes argued that case studies are simulations of real life, but I do not understand the rationale for saying this. Case studies set scenarios with which a skilled teacher can engage students and elicit arguments from them. It is through these arguments that learning takes place. A good case study does not necessarily have an obvious or a unique solution.

But case studies can also be used differently. They can be presented to show how clever the teacher is. Or they can be employed to show how important a particular theory could be without any reflection.

They can also be used to simply create pressure, especially in the case of the long 30 or 40 page Harvard Business School case studies. Applied in this way they are not intellectually challenging. In these instances case studies are merely a teaching convenience.

In the sense that case studies are a teaching convenience they are largely all the same. The case study normally requires the student to sort through a large about of information or data in order to find the salient facts that are required to understand the case. I have heard Harvard professors proudly state that they write their case studies like mystery stories to test the ability of the student to sort the wheat from the chaff. Once the important facts have been identified then, in the way case studies were taught to our class, the case should be all but cracked. But this is not necessarily how it works in real life. My impression is that what we learnt was rather simplistic.

## UCT graduation

Graduation took place in the middle of December. It was a grand occasion as these events always are. Jameson Hall was packed with bright young faces being launched into the wide world and proud parents abounded.

I picked up my degree certificate made my farewells to what were now my former class-mates and I headed north. On my trip south I had been able to easily fit all my worldly possessions into my old close- to-clapped-out Austin Cambridge but now I struggled to fit everything into the car. The books, the lever arch files, the boxes of papers and the other paraphernalia I had accumulated filled the vehicle completely.

I was very pleased to be free of the UCT Graduate School of Business. I had felt trapped there as I realised that I could not walk away and say what a dreadful place it was as no one would have believed me. As far as I was concerned I had been let down by the University and I wanted to put this entire unfortunate episode behind me.

I was of course sad to be leaving Cape Town as I would have preferred to have lived there instead of the Reef, but the business potential in the North was much greater and my financial resources were now really quite low, so I had to find employment relatively quickly. On this trip North it was not necessary to avail myself of the hospitality of the police station in Beaufort West.

## Finding a job

Having an MBA was certainly an assistance in finding a job, but nonetheless it took me about 6 six weeks to so do. I had been earning R500.00 a month when I gave up my position at the end of 1971 and I now started my new job at R750.00. I was also able to find a part-time lecturing position at a private college teaching management accounting as well as economics. As a result within six months I was able to pay back my bank loan and replace my old even-closer-to-clapped-out motor vehicle with another old, but not so clapped out car.

I never looked back financially.

## The Rabbit Hole

I have always felt that the style of the UCT Business School regime was unfair for several reasons.

In the first place they seemed to oversell what they actually had to offer. All the propaganda about the latest thinking from overseas and the highly skilled and experienced international faculty was, being charitable, exaggerated.

The decision of the gifted teacher with the national reputation to re-place himself with a tape recorder was truly amazing.

Using the fear of being thrown off the programme as a motivator was not acceptable.

The telegram method of informing a student that he or she had been axed was highly unpleasant and unnecessary.

The draconian regime which did not treat the students as adult men and women and which locked doors at 08.00 was not really neces-sary.

And so on.

I guess due to my particular business background and the subjects which I had taken as an undergraduate I learnt little from the pro-gramme.

So what did I learn:-

I learnt that I could work 80 hours a week or more, week-in and week-out. Forty hour weeks had something to do with political considerations, but had nothing to do with the physical capability of motivated men and women;

I learnt that I could produce a report with zero errors and I could submit it on time when it was necessary;

I learnt that I could survive a draconian regime by keeping my head down and getting on with the job at hand;

I learnt that sometimes 08.00 does not mean 08.01;

I learnt that group work can be essential, but I also learnt that groups can also waste a lot of time if they are not focused on the job in the right way;

I learnt that I could hold my own in a group of 86 people who were supposed to be special and were expected to become the future leaders of South African industry.

A question which I ask myself is, "Would I do this degree again?" The answer is *Yes,* but I would like to have known what the culture of the institution was before signing up. I could have been emotionally better prepared for what was an ordeal.

## Final reflections

To emphasise a point made earlier the MBA seemed to have most benefit for the engineers and the scientists and to those who had no previous formal business education. To

69

others much of the academic content was rather low level. For this reason I have heard the MBA described as a sort of superficial Bachelor of Commerce degree completed in one year. This is a harsh judgement, but it is true to say that the academic content of an MBA may not necessarily match that of a three year bachelor degree. Of course, some would say that thinking only of the academic content may be regarded as unfortunate as it does not take into account the other aspects of a quite complex event. The question then becomes, *To what extent should a university be concerned with the non-academic issues involved with the degree?* There is an interesting debate as to whether universities should see its mandate as creating "job ready individuals". But except for professions which are well defined and perhaps regulated it can be difficult to be confident as to what would constitute a job ready individual. What would make someone job ready could vary enormously.

From the point of view of the educational process I have no idea whether the happenings of 1972 were typical of how the UCT MBA has been run since then. It may have been quite unique and on the other hand it may not. Either way I think that this story is worth telling and it is certainly worth thinking about how an MBA should be conducted.

Universities are generally not particularly self-critical of the quality of the education and the service they deliver. Even when there are formal channels for feedback it is not always listened to attentively. There is sometimes the perception that students will be critical in order to reduce their workload and to obtain the highest grade level. There is also the fact that students may mistakenly believe that they know better than the faculty. The dialogue between students and faculty is often delicate and complex. Sometimes the faculty just get it wrong and they do not deliver what was promised. But students do not see it as being in their interests to broadcast the inadequacy or the limitations of the degree they have been awarded. There has been an effective code of silence. A senior colleague of mine from a famous European university described this as *the great university conspiracy*. Perhaps it is time for this to change? Maybe the current phenomenon in the UK whereby universities are being sued by their students much more frequently than even before is the beginning of the end of the code of silence.

There are several other questions which have bothered me over the years.

Was it really necessary to conduct the MBA under such a draconian regime? Is fear of expulsion a good motivator in the education environment? It is sometimes said that the only way to motivate people is through the combination of the carrot and the stick. But this idea is at best a crude over-simplification of human nature and it contradicts much of what the School was teaching in its Human Relations and Behaviour module.

Would members of the class not have learnt more if the School had been more supportive of them? How different would it have been if Professor Boland had opened the first session of the year with a statement that it was the intention of the School to support everyone so that they would be able to develop their potential to the full and in so doing master the material presented and thus become educated, reflective, and potentially accomplished managers? Would this not have been the proper ethos for a university?

Was it necessary to inundate us with so much work? I feel that the idea of deep learning is sometime over stated but at UCT it seemed to be entirely unknown. An excessive workload can become toxic to the learning process.

Was one American case study after another the only way of conveying useful knowledge? Case studies can be a way of reducing the preparation effort required by the faculty and transferring it to the student.

Was the telegram dismissal device appropriate? I cannot help but feel that there was a moral issue implied in sending a telegram to someone who was living only a dozen metres away from the School administrative offices.

Should there not have been an appeal from dismissal from the programme, especially when it was not possible to re-sit an exam?

Should a degree have been awarded to someone who has failed two of the 14 courses required?

Should the professor have been allowed to replace himself with a tape recorder and a few exercises and some multiple choice books?

Should the same case studies have been used for examinations in subsequent years?

What responsibility did the Vice-Chancellor and his top team on the Upper Campus have for what went on at the Graduate School of Business on the Lower Campus?

But at the end of the day in the almost 50 years since its inauguration the School has had thousands of graduates who have benefited enormously from their experience and who will no doubt continue to so do. Nonetheless it is worth thinking about the nature of an MBA and how it should be delivered. I hope that this story stimulates such a discussion.